First Science

Keep it Afloat!

Editorial planning: Serpentine Editorial
Scientific consultant: Dr. J.J.M. Rowe

Designed by The R & B Partnership
Illustrator: David Anstey
Photographer: Peter Millard

Additional photographs:
Chris Fairclough Colour Library 10, 12;
ZEFA 11, 14, 20, 22, 29, 30 (top), 31 (top);
G I Bernard/NHPA 30 (bottom).

Library of Congress Cataloging-in-Publication Data

Rowe, Julian.
   Keep it afloat! / by Julian Rowe and Molly Perham.
      p. cm. — (First science)
   Includes index.
   Summary: Describes in simple terms why some things float and some sink.
   ISBN 0-516-08134-9
   1. Hydrostatics — Experiments — Juvenile literature. [1. Floating bodies —
Experiments. 2. Experiments.] I. Perham, Molly. II. Title. III. Series: First science
(Chicago, Ill.)
   QC147.5.R69 1993
   532'.2'078—dc20   93-8213
                                                                          CIP
                                                                          AC

1993 Childrens Press® Edition
© 1993 Watts Books, London
All rights reserved. Printed in the United States of America.
1 2 3 4 5 6 7 8 9 10 R 02 01 00 99 98 97 96 95 94 93

First Science

Keep it Afloat!

Julian Rowe
and Molly Perham

CHILDRENS PRESS®
CHICAGO

Contents

FLOATERS AND SINKERS page 6

TEST IT OUT page 8

BOATS AFLOAT page 10

CARGO SHIPS page 12

WATER PUSHES BACK page 14

LEARNING TO SWIM page 16

UNDER THE WATER page 18

 SUBMARINES page 20

LIGHTER THAN WATER page 22

 OIL AND WATER page 24

SOAPY WATER
page 26

FLOATING ON AIR
page 28

THINK ABOUT...
FLOATING page 30

INDEX page 32

 SAFETY WARNING

Activities marked with this symbol require the presence and
help of an adult. Plastic should always be used instead of glass.
Take special care near water.

Floaters and sinkers

This girl is sailing her boat in a pool.
It floats on the water.
A puff of wind fills
the sail and takes
the boat to the
other side.

Have you ever thrown a pebble into a pool?
It sinks straight to the bottom. All you see
is a circle of ripples on the surface
of the pool.

Test it out

Which things float and which things sink?
How can you find out?

This boy is collecting all kinds of things
to test. Some of them
are natural objects
such as a lemon,
shells, a cork, and a
pine cone. Others
are household
objects.

You can use a plastic fish tank or a large bowl to test things. See how the marbles and the shells have sunk to the bottom. Which things are floating on the top?

The lemon floats because the peel contains tiny pockets of air. Why does the peeled lemon sink?

Boats afloat

Inside the hull of a sailboat there are hollow spaces filled with air. These keep the boat from sinking if it is blown over or capsizes.

A giant passenger ship is very heavy.
It weighs as much as a big building.

But it floats because, like the sailboat,
its hull is hollow and contains air.

Cargo ships

This ship carries thousands of tons of cargo. The heavy containers are carefully loaded so that the ship does not tip over and sink.

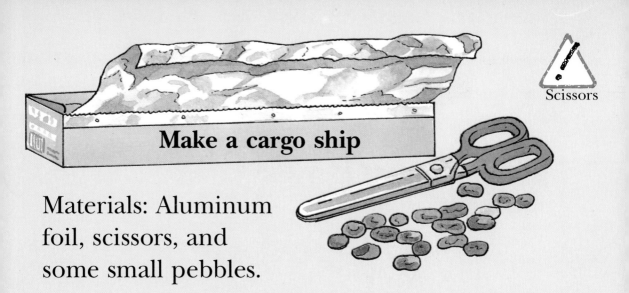

Make a cargo ship

Materials: Aluminum foil, scissors, and some small pebbles.

Cut a piece of foil the size of this page. Bend up the edges on each side.

Fold the corners so that water cannot get in.

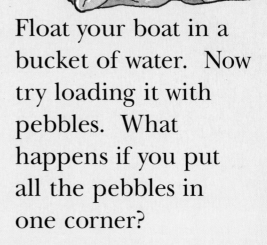

Float your boat in a bucket of water. Now try loading it with pebbles. What happens if you put all the pebbles in one corner?

water pushes back

Have you ever paddled an inflatable boat? Why do you think it floats so easily in the water?

When you push the paddle through the water, can you feel the water pushing back?

This big ball is full of air. It floats on top of the water. If you try to sink it, you can feel the water pushing back.

Learning to swim

Have you ever played with a beach ball in the water?

If you hold onto the ball, it will keep you afloat.

This girl is learning to swim. Her armbands are full of air. They are called water wings. They keep her afloat.

Under the water

Plants that live under water have pockets
of air inside them. These air pockets
keep the plants floating in the water.

Fish have a built-in floating aid, called a swim bladder, inside their bodies. They can control the amount of air in the swim bladder. This allows them to float higher or lower in the water.

Submarines

A submarine rises up and sinks down in the water like a fish.

When it dives, air is pumped out of its ballast tanks and water comes in. When the water is blown out, the submarine rises.

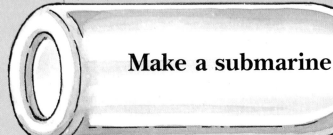

Make a submarine

Materials: A plastic bottle, plastic tubing, and some modeling clay.

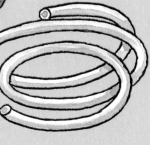

Make a hole in the bottom of the bottle. Cover it with modeling clay.

Make a hole in the cap. Push the piece of plastic tubing through it.

Fill the bottle with water. Screw the cap back on.

Put your submarine under water in a large bowl or tank. Remove the modeling clay.

Now blow down the tube and watch your submarine rise to the surface.

Lighter than water

Some things float because they are lighter than water. Ice is lighter than water.

Huge icebergs float in the seas around the North Pole.

Make an iceberg

Materials: An empty yogurt container. Fill it with water and put it in the freezer.

When the water has frozen, hold the yogurt container under running water until the ice inside loosens. Take out the block of ice.

Put your iceberg in a bowl of water. How much is under the water?

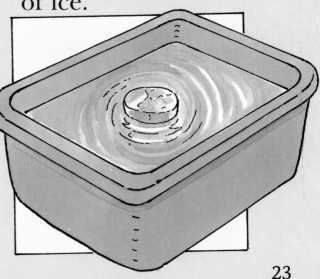

Oil and water

Oil is lighter than water. It spreads out on the surface of the water. When it rains, you can see oily patterns in puddles on the street.

If a tanker spills some oil at sea, the oil spreads far and wide. It does not mix with the water.

Make oily pictures

Materials: Oil paints, turpentine, an oven pan, heavy construction paper, and an old fork.

Turpentine

Fill the pan with water, and add a spoonful of turpentine.

Add some drops of oil paint to the water.

Stir the colors around with the fork to make a pattern.

Carefully lay the paper flat on the water. Lift the paper quickly and let the water drip off. Tack your picture up to dry.

Soapy water

Oil mixes with water if detergent is added. These children are washing greasy plates using a detergent.

When seabirds swim in oily water, the oil sticks to their feathers. The oil can be removed with a detergent, which is then washed away.

Mixing oil and water

Materials: A clean empty bottle with a screw cap, dishwashing liquid, and cooking oil.

Put some oil in the bottle.

Half-fill the bottle with water. See how the oil rises to the top.

Add a few drops of dishwashing liquid.

Now screw the cap onto the bottle and give it a good shake. What has happened to the oil?

Floating on air

Just as some liquids are lighter than water, some gases are lighter than air. This boy is holding balloons filled with helium gas. Helium is lighter than air, so the balloons float.

Hot-air balloons float because the warm air inside them is lighter than the cold air outside.

Think about... floating

Ducks spend most of their day floating on water. The quills of their feathers are hollow and contain air.

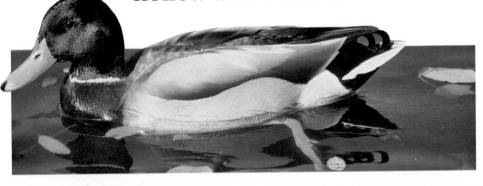

Giant coconuts float for hundreds of miles from one island to another in the Pacific Ocean. These seeds then grow into new trees.

What is the easiest way to move heavy logs?
In Canada, huge rafts of logs are pulled by
tugboat to the sawmill.

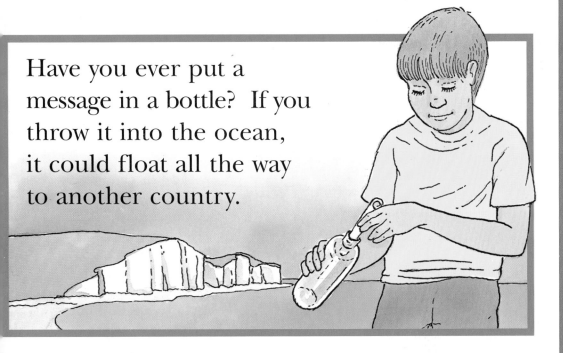

Have you ever put a
message in a bottle? If you
throw it into the ocean,
it could float all the way
to another country.

INDEX

air, 9, 10, 11, 15, 17, 18, 19, 20, 28, 29, 30
armbands, 17
ball, 15, 16
ballast tank, 20
balloons, 28
boat, 6, 14
bottle, 31
cargo, 12, 13
cargo ship, 12, 13
coconuts, 30
containers, 12
cork, 8
detergent, 26, 27
ducks, 30
feathers, 26, 30
fish, 19
gases, 28
helium gas, 28
hot-air balloons, 29
hull, 10, 11
ice, 22
iceberg, 22, 23
inflatable boat, 14
lemon, 8, 9
logs, 31
marbles, 9
oil, 24, 26, 27
paddle, 14
paints, 25
passenger ship, 11
pebble, 7
pine cone, 8
plants, 18
pockets of air, 9, 18
puddle, 24
quills, 30
rain, 24
ripples, 7
sail, 6
sailboat, 10, 11
seabirds, 26
shells, 8, 9
ship, 11
sponge, 8, 9
submarine, 20, 21
swim bladder, 19
swimming, 17
tank, 9
tanker, 24
tugboat, 31
water wings, 17